GRAPHIC SCIENCE

THE WHIRLWIND WORLD OF HURRICANES

WITH **MAX AXIOM** ®
SUPER SCIENTIST

by Katherine Krohn

illustrated by Cynthia Martin and Al Milgrom

Consultant:
Matt Smith
Senior Research Scientist
University of Alabama in Huntsville

CAPSTONE PRESS
a capstone imprint

Graphic Library is published by Capstone Press,
1710 Roe Crest Drive, North Mankato, Minnesota 56003.
www.capstonepub.com

Library of Congress Cataloging-in-Publication Data
Krohn, Katherine E.
  The whirlwind world of hurricanes with Max Axiom, super scientist / by Katherine Krohn.
    p. cm. — (Graphic library. Graphic science)
  Summary: "In graphic novel format, follows the adventures of Max Axiom as he explores
the science and history behind hurricanes"—Provided by publisher.
  ISBN 978-1-4296-4773-1 (library binding)
  ISBN 978-1-4296-5636-8 (paperback)
  1. Hurricanes—Juvenile literature. 2. Adventure stories. I. Title. II. Series.

QC944.2.K76 2011
551.55'2—dc22   2010006563

Designer
Alison Thiele

Colorist
Krista Ward

Media Researcher
Wanda Winch

Production Specialist
Laura Manthe

Editor
Mari Bolte

Printed in China.
0812/CA21201120
072012   006865R

TABLE of CONTENTS

Hurricanes form in the summer and fall when the sun is especially warm over tropical ocean waters.

They form close to the equator, where water temperatures are warmest.

Warm, moist air rises over the warm ocean waters and creates thunderstorms. A rising column of wind comes up in the center of the storm and spins in a spiral shape.

OUTWARD-FLOWING WIND

HUMID AIR

OUTSIDE WINDS

RISING WIND

WARM OCEAN WATERS

The storm gains power and speed as it spins. As the storm spins faster, it grows more powerful. Let's take a closer look!

SPEEDY STORMS

ACCESS GRANTED: MAX AXIOM

A storm goes through a series of changes before becoming a hurricane. During the first stage, called a tropical depression, winds begin to rotate. Wind speeds reach 23 to 38 miles (37 to 61 kilometers) per hour. Then it turns into a tropical storm. During this stage, the storm becomes more organized and starts to resemble a hurricane. Wind speeds reach 39 to 73 mph (63 to 117 kph). When winds reach speeds of 74 mph (119 kph), the storm is finally called a hurricane.

7

This storm surge only damaged property. In the end, the hurricane's winds took out power lines. The heavy rainfall flooded neighborhoods. The small storm surge damaged buildings. This time, no lives were lost.

Scientists are getting better at measuring and predicting hurricanes. They save many lives by warning people who live in the path of a hurricane.

Let's talk with a hurricane specialist at the National Hurricane Center in Miami.

We gather as much information as possible about a storm. This information helps determine the size, speed, and path of a hurricane.

0800

There are scientists who collect data about tropical storms. They fly into hurricanes on a regular basis.

Let me introduce you to some of them.

THE SAFFIR-SIMPSON SCALE

ACCESS GRANTED: MAX AXIOM

The Saffir-Simpson Scale was developed by scientists Herbert Saffir and Bob Simpson in the 1970s. Saffir realized that no simple scale existed that could measure the likely effects of a hurricane. He created the wind speed portion of the scale. Later, Simpson added the barometric pressure and storm surge measurements.

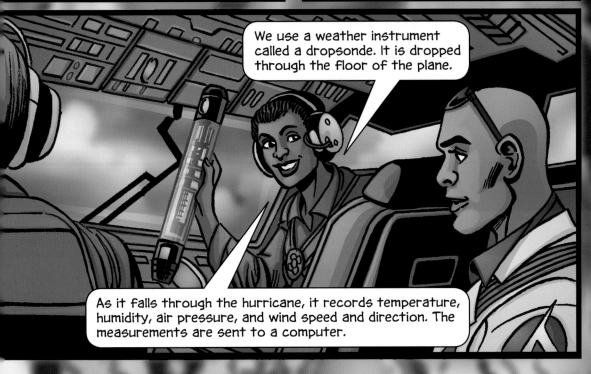

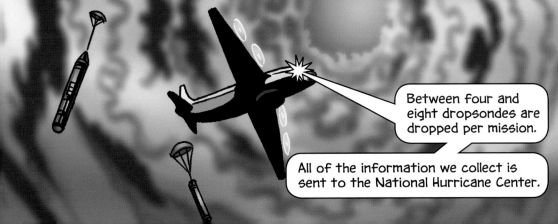

One of the worst hurricanes in U.S. history took place on September 8, 1900. A fierce category 4 hurricane swept through the city of Galveston, Texas.

The 15-foot, or 4.6-meter, storm surge and 135-mile, or 217-kilometer, per hour winds destroyed the city.

Storm prediction methods were not advanced in 1900. The people of Galveston received almost no warning. The hurricane left many people homeless, and thousands dead.

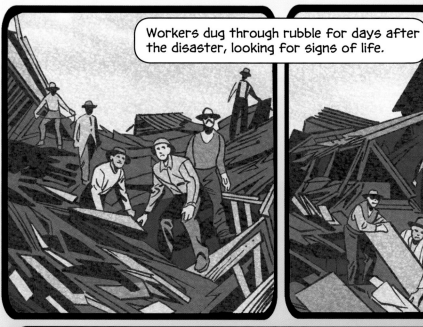

Workers dug through rubble for days after the disaster, looking for signs of life.

The storm did more than $20 million in damage. That would be $510 million today!

The Galveston hurricane was the most deadly natural disaster in United States history.

More than 6,000 people were killed in the storm.

In 1992 Hurricane Andrew swirled across the Atlantic Ocean. Andrew began as a tropical wave off the coast of Africa. As it moved westward, it developed into a category 5 hurricane.

COMPOSITE OF ANDREW
23 Aug 92-09 UTC
to
26 Aug 92-09 UTC

Hurricane Andrew first hit the northwestern Bahamas. Next the town of Homestead, in southern Florida, was hit. Andrew continued on to strike parts of Louisiana.

In Louisiana power lines were knocked down. More than 152,000 people were without power.

The hurricane damaged the city's pipes. As a result, the tap water was unclean. Residents had to boil their drinking water.

Hurricane Andrew created 165-mile, or 266-kilometer, per hour winds. At such high speeds, seemingly harmless pieces of wood and metal become flying missiles.

National Guard troops were called in to southern Florida. Their job was to protect businesses and homes from looters, or thieves.

The looters included some of the 250,000 people left homeless by the hurricane.

Hurricane Andrew killed at least 65 people and caused more than $25 billion in damages.

A few years later another killer hurricane would swirl across the Atlantic Ocean. It caused an even worse disaster than Hurricane Andrew.

The largest natural disaster in U.S. history began as a Category I hurricane. It formed over the Bahamas on August 23, 2005. Officials named the storm Katrina.

The storm peaked in power on August 28 and came ashore in southeastern Louisiana the next day. The storm hit the coasts of Louisiana, Mississippi, and Alabama very hard. The mayor of New Orleans ordered people to evacuate the city.

New Orleans had a system of levees, or floodwalls. They were built to protect the city from flooding. But the levees failed. The city began to flood.

KATRINA'S DEADLY PATH

ACCESS GRANTED: MAX AXIOM

After forming over the Bahamas, Katrina crossed southern Florida as a Category 1 hurricane. It built strength and speed over the Gulf of Mexico. It slammed into New Orleans on August 29 as a Category 3 hurricane. It continued on to the coast of Mississippi, where it finally wound down on August 30. The strong winds from the hurricane also led to 62 tornadoes in eight states.

Despite the mayor's order, nearly 100,000 people stayed in the city. Some chose not to leave, but others simply did not have a way to get out. After the storm, they were fighting for their lives. By August 31, most of New Orleans was flooded. Some areas were under up to 15 feet, or 4.6 meters, of water.

Hurricane Katrina caused about $75 billion in damage. It was the most expensive disaster in U.S. history.

The hurricane killed more than 1,800 people in Florida, Louisiana, and Mississippi.

Hurricanes such as Andrew and Katrina will be remembered in the history books. But how did these powerful storms get their names in the first place?

Hi, Tam! What can you tell me about hurricane names?

Hundreds of years ago, the people of the West Indies began naming hurricanes, or cyclones, after saints.

A massive cyclone tore through Puerto Rico on July 26, 1825. The saint known as Santa Ana is celebrated on July 26. As a result, the cyclone was named Santa Ana.

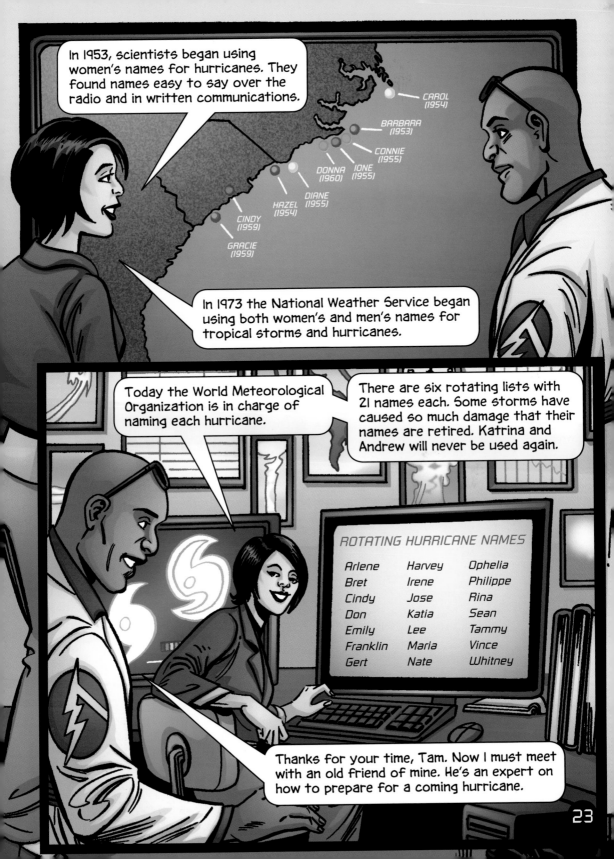

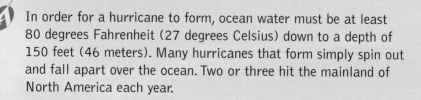

MORE ABOUT HURRICANES

In order for a hurricane to form, ocean water must be at least 80 degrees Fahrenheit (27 degrees Celsius) down to a depth of 150 feet (46 meters). Many hurricanes that form simply spin out and fall apart over the ocean. Two or three hit the mainland of North America each year.

The official hurricane season over the Atlantic Ocean runs from June through November. The Pacific Ocean season is from mid-May through November. Activity in both oceans peaks from mid-August to late October.

In past years, scientists experimented with dropping chemicals into tropical storms to break the storms apart. This is no longer attempted because of a lack of funding and the ethical questions it creates.

A tropical storm's size has nothing to do with its strength. Sometimes a small storm can be very destructive and dangerous.

According to the National Hurricane Center, Florida has been hit with the most hurricanes. Sixty hurricanes came ashore in Florida between 1900 and 2000.

All tropical storms spin counterclockwise in the Northern Hemisphere. They spin clockwise in the Southern Hemisphere.

The National Science Foundation did an investigation after Hurricane Katrina. They found design flaws in New Orleans' levees. They also found that the levees had not been maintained properly.

The U.S. military unofficially began using women's names to identify hurricanes during World War II. Soldiers named the storms after their wives or girlfriends.

 Unlike typical thuderstorms over land, storms in and around a hurricane's eye wall do not contain much lightning.

 Hurricanes are known as cyclones in the Bay of Bengal and northern Indian Ocean. The same type of weather system is called a typhoon in the western Pacific Ocean. Near Australia, it's known as a willy-willy.

MORE ABOUT

SUPER SCIENTIST

Real name: **Maxwell J. Axiom**
Hometown: **Seattle, Washington**
Height: **6' 1"**   Weight: **192 lbs**
Eyes: **Brown**   Hair: **None**

Super capabilities: Super intelligence; able to shrink to the size of an atom; sunglasses give x-ray vision; lab coat allows for travel through time and space.

Origin: Since birth, Max Axiom seemed destined for greatness. His mother, a marine biologist, taught her son about the mysteries of the sea. His father, a nuclear physicist and volunteer park ranger, schooled Max on the wonders of earth and sky.

One day on a wilderness hike, a megacharged lightning bolt struck Max with blinding fury. When he awoke, Max discovered a newfound energy and set out to learn as much about science as possible. He traveled the globe earning degrees in every aspect of the field. Upon his return, he was ready to share his knowledge and new identity with the world. He had become Max Axiom, Super Scientist.

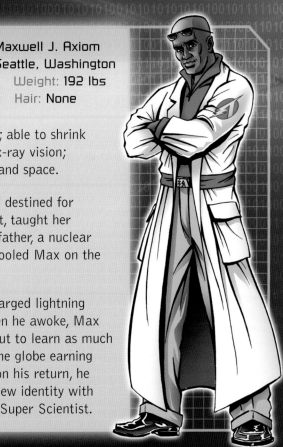

GLOSSARY

barometric pressure (buh-RAH-meh-TRIK PRESH-ur)—changes in air pressure; barometric pressure is measured by a barometer

dropsonde (DROP-sahnd)—an information collecting device used to obtain information related to hurricanes and weather prediction

evacuate (i-VA-kyuh-wayt)—to leave an area during a time of danger

eye (EYE)—the central, calm area at the center of a hurricane

eye wall (EYE WAHL)—the tall, vertical wall of fast-moving clouds lining the outer edge of a hurricane's eye

levee (LEH-vee)—a long, continuous wall that protects a coastal area from flooding

meteorologist (mee-tee-ur-AWL-uh-jist)—a person who studies and predicts the weather

rain band (RAYN band)—a spiral arc of thunderstorms around tropical storms, especially hurricanes

Saffir-Simpson Scale (SAF-fir SIMP-suhn SKALE)—a scale from one to five that rates a hurricane based on its wind speed; the scale helps experts guess how much damage and flooding the hurricane might cause

storm surge (STORM SURJ)—a sudden, strong rush of water that happens as a hurricane moves onto land

tropical depression (TRAH-pu-kuhl di-PRE-shuhn)—ocean thunderstorm having winds of less than 39 mph (63 kph)

tropical storm (TRAH-pu-kuhl STORM)—ocean thunderstorm having winds from 39 to 73 mph (63 to 117 kph)

READ MORE

Jeffrey, Gary. *Hurricane Hunters & Tornado Chasers.* Graphic Careers. New York: Rosen Central, 2008.

Longshore, David. *Encyclopedia of Hurricanes, Typhoons, and Cyclones.* Facts on File Science Library. New York: Facts on File, 2008.

Nardo, Don. *Storm Surge: The Science of Hurricanes.* Headline Science. Mankato, Minn.: Compass Point Books, 2009.

Treaster, Joseph B. *Hurricane Force: In the Path of America's Deadliest Storms.* Boston: Kingfisher, 2007.

INTERNET SITES

FactHound offers a safe, fun way to find Internet sites related to this book. All sites on FactHound have been researched by our staff.

Here's all you do:

Visit *www.facthound.com*

Type in this code: 9781429647731